Music Minus One Vocals

BROADWAY HITS

for Mezzo Soprano

T0056449

2143

BROADWAY HITS
for Mezzo Soprano

CONTENTS

ISBN 978-1-941566-43-5

MMO 2143

The Simple Joys Of Maidenhood

from "Camelot"

Words and Music by
Alan Jay Lerner and Frederick Loewe

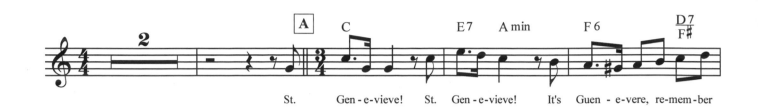

Many A New Day

from "Oklahoma!"

Words and Music by
Oscar Hammerstein II and Richard Rodgers

Why should a wo-man who is health-y and strong, blub-ber like a ba-by if her

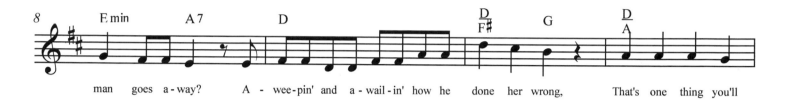

man goes a-way? A - wee-pin' and a-wail-in' how he done her wrong, That's one thing you'll

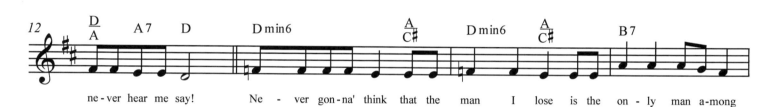

ne-ver hear me say! Ne - ver gon-na' think that the man I lose is the on-ly man a-mong

men. I'll snap my fin-gers to show I don't care, I'll buy me a brand new

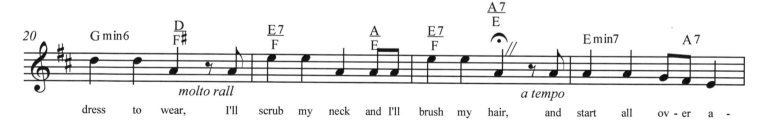

molto rall   *a tempo*

dress to wear, I'll scrub my neck and I'll brush my hair, and start all ov-er a-

gain. _____   1. Ma-ny a new face will please my eye, Ma-ny a new love will find me;

(chorus) 2. Ma-ny a new face will please my eye, Ma-ny a new love will find me;

Goodnight, My Someone

from "The Music Man"

Words and Music by
Meredith Willson

Ribbons Down My Back

from "Hello, Dolly!"

Words and Music by
Jerry Herman

Before I Gaze At You Again

from "Camelot"

Words and Music by
Alan Jay Lerner and Frederick Loewe

MMO 2143

I'm Gonna Wash That Man Right Outta My Hair

from "South Pacific"

Words and Music by
Oscar Hammerstein II and
Richard Rodgers

MMO 2143

15

MMO 2143

You'll Never Walk Alone

from "Carousel"

**Words and Music by
Oscar Hammerstein II and Richard Rodgers**

Can't Help Lovin' Dat Man

from "Show Boat"

Words and Music by
Oscar Hammerstein II and
Jerome Kern

MMO 2143

I Put My Hand In

from "Hello, Dolly!"

Words and Music by
Jerry Herman

Other Great Vocals from Music Minus One

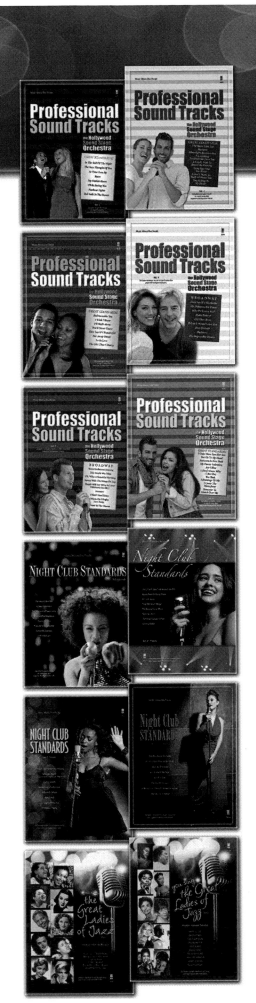

Professional Sound Tracks, Vol. 1 ....MMO 2121
In The Still Of The Night • The Very Thought Of You • As Time Goes By • Yours • My Foolish Heart • I'll Be Seeing You • Harbour Lights • Red Sails In The Sunset

Professional Sound Tracks, Vol. 2 ....MMO 2122
The More I See You • Stardust • Moonlight Becomes You • I'm Getting Sentimental Over You • A Lovely Way To Spend An Evening • Long Ago And Far Away • I Don't Want To Walk Without You • You Belong To My Heart

Professional Sound Tracks, Vol. 3 ....MMO 2123
Embraceable You • I Wish I Knew • I'll Walk Alone • You'll Never Know • They Say It's Wonderful • Born Again • So In Love • The Girl That I Marry

Professional Sound Tracks, Vol. 4 ....MMO 2124
They Say It's Wonderful • My Defenses Are Down • Why Do I Love You? • Make Believe • Old Man River • If Ever I Would Leave You • Don Quixote (Man of La Mancha) • Dulcinea (Man of La Mancha) • The Impossible Dream (Man of La Mancha)

Professional Sound Tracks, Vol. 5 ....MMO 2125
Some Enchanted Evening • This Nearly Was Mine • Oh, What a Beautiful Morning • Surrey With The Fringe On Top • People Will Say We're In Love /Oklahoma • Memory • I Won't Send Roses • (Where Do I Begin) Love Story • Send In The Clowns

Professional Sound Tracks, Vol. 6 ....MMO 2126
I Only Have Eyes For You • You Go To My Head • Autumn In New York • My Funny Valentine • Am I Blue • I Don't Know Why (I Just Do) • You Took Advantage Of Me • I Cover The Waterfront • Someone To Watch Over Me

Night Club Standards, Vol. 1 (Female) ....MMO 2131
The More I See You • It Had to Be You • The Shadow of Your Smile • Watch What Happens • The Good Life • Call Me Irresponsible • Street of Dreams • I Should Care

Night Club Standards, Vol. 2 (Female) ....MMO 2132
They Can't Take That Away From Me • Come Rain Or Come Shine • Nice 'N' Easy • That Old Black Magic • It's Only A Paper Moon • Summer Wind • The Very Thought Of You • My Baby Just Cares for Me

Night Club Standards, Vol. 3 (Female) ....MMO 2133
I've Got The World On A String • Saturday Night (Is The Loneliest Night Of The Week • It's De-Lovely • Something's Gotta Give • Where Or When • Witchcraft • I Thought About You • Without A Song

Night Club Standards, Vol. 4 (Female) ....MMO 2134
The Best Is Yet To Come • I Could Have Danced All Night • They All Laughed • Oh, Look At Me Now • If I Had You • I'm Old Fashioned • A Nightingale Sang In Berkeley Square • The Lady Is A Tramp

The Great Ladies Of Jazz, Vol. 1 ....MMO 2135
A Good Man Is Hard To Find • Guess Who's In Town • Rockin' Chair • A Hundred Years From Today • It Don't Mean A Thing • Lullaby Of The Leaves • Goody Goody • Guess Who I Saw Today • What Is This Thing Called Love? • Moments Like This

The Great Ladies Of Jazz, Vol. 2 ....MMO 2136
Take The 'A; Train • Million Dollar Secret • Day Dream • Cried For You • Maybe • Too Late Now • Peel Me A Grape • Blue Gardenia • Street of Dreams • All That Jazz

Music Minus One
50 Executive Boulevard • Elmsford, New York 10523-1325
914-592-1188 • e-mail: info@musicminusone.com
www.musicminusone.com

MMO 2143

ISBN 978-1-941566-43-5